CW01024013

Luca Petrov

Ecuador
Travel Guide

Catalog

Cultural Marvels

Ecuador: A Tapestry of Nature and Heritage

While Paris may boast its charm, Ecuador's captivating cities, including Quito, Cuenca, and Guayaquil, stand as testaments to the country's rich cultural tapestry. Rooted in ancient civilizations like the Incas, Ecuador unfolds as a treasure trove of history, art, and natural wonders. Prepare to immerse yourself in the unique masterpieces that have shaped Ecuador's diverse cultural heritage.

Quito: City of Volcanoes and Heritage

Quito, surrounded by volcanic landscapes, offers a blend of historic charm and modern allure. Explore the colonial wonders of the Old Town, visit the impressive Basilica del Voto Nacional, and delve into the indigenous marketplaces for a taste of Ecuador's vibrant traditions.

Cuenca: Artistic Hub of the Andes

Cuenca, often hailed as the "Artistic Hub of the Andes," showcases indigenous artistry alongside colonial architecture. Wander through the cobbled streets, marvel at the beauty of Cuenca's cathedrals, and discover local crafts that echo centuries-old techniques.

Guayaquil: Gateway to the Pacific

Guayaquil, Ecuador's bustling port city, pulsates with energy. Stroll along the Malecon 2000, explore the historic neighborhood of Las Peñas, and witness the city's commitment to contemporary art in its numerous galleries.

Ecuador's cultural treasures extend beyond its cities. Explore the ancient mysteries of Ingapirca, marvel at the intricate craftsmanship of the Chordeleg silverware, and witness the vibrant colors of indigenous markets in Otavalo.

Vibrant Vida

In Ecuador, the dance of life unfolds seamlessly, where tradition and modernity coalesce. A symphony of indigenous rituals, contemporary art scenes, and gastronomic brilliance creates a kaleidoscope of experiences.
Ecuadorians have mastered the art of living, evident in the vibrant festivals, the pulse of urban life, and the fusion of traditional textiles with modern fashion. Embrace the "vida vibrante" – the vibrant life – as you slow down to savor every moment of Ecuador's unique cultural blend.

Sabor delicioso

Ecuador, often referred to as the heart of South America, is a feast for the senses. From savory ceviche on the coast to hearty locro in the highlands, each bite introduces you to the rich culinary heritage shaped by diverse ecosystems. The essence of Ecuadorian cuisine lies in fresh, locally sourced ingredients and a celebration of seasonal flavors. Whether you're savoring coastal delicacies in Manta, exploring the markets of Ambato, or indulging in the aromatic flavors of Amazonian dishes, be prepared for a culinary journey that mirrors the country's geographical diversity.

Lush Landscapes

Ecuador's allure extends far beyond its cultural marvels. Nature herself has adorned the country with a breathtaking array of landscapes, from the majestic Andes to the lush Amazon rainforest and the pristine Galápagos Islands.
Embark on a thrilling adventure as you hike the Quilotoa Loop, explore the biodiversity of the Yasuní National Park, or marvel at the unique wildlife on the Galápagos. Ecuador's landscapes promise a tapestry of outdoor experiences, as diverse and awe-inspiring as the cultural treasures that define this remarkable country.

1. Galápagos Islands:

- **History:** The Galápagos Islands, located in the Pacific Ocean, are renowned for their unique biodiversity. Formed by volcanic activity, these islands played a crucial role in Charles Darwin's development of the theory of evolution. Named a UNESCO World Heritage site, the Galápagos have been inhabited intermittently, with their delicate ecosystems carefully preserved to maintain the incredible diversity of species that inspired Darwin's groundbreaking work.
- **Key Attractions:** Explore unique wildlife, including giant tortoises, marine iguanas, and blue-footed boobies. Diving and snorkeling opportunities are abundant.
- **When to Visit:** Year-round, but June to December is optimal for wildlife observation.

- **Contact Info**: Galápagos National Park: +593 5-252-8011, [Official Website](http://www.galapagospark.org/)
- **Hidden Gems:** Visit Genovesa Island for birdwatching, especially the red-footed booby colonies.

2. Quito:

- **History**: Quito, Ecuador's capital, was founded by the Spanish in the 16th century on the ruins of an Incan city. Its historic center, known for its well-preserved colonial architecture, was declared a UNESCO World Heritage site. Quito has been a cultural and political hub, witnessing the shifts from indigenous civilizations to Spanish colonial rule and eventually becoming part of independent Ecuador.
- **Key Attractions**: Quito's Old Town, Basilica del Voto Nacional, and the Middle of the World monument.
- **When to Visit:** All year round, with June to September being the dry season.

- **Contact Info:** Quito Tourism Board: +593 2-397-1500, [Official Website](http://www.quito.com.ec/)
- **Culinary Delights:** Try locro de papa (potato soup) at traditional markets.

3. Cuenca:

- **History:** Established in 1557 by the Spanish, Cuenca is steeped in colonial history. With its well-preserved architecture, including cathedrals and cobbled streets, Cuenca became a UNESCO World Heritage site. It played a pivotal role in Ecuador's fight for independence, and today, its rich cultural heritage is celebrated through various festivals and events.
- **Key Attractions**: Cuenca's Historic Center, New Cathedral, and the Tomebamba River.
- **When to Visit:** Best from September to November during the dry season.
- **Contact Info:** Cuenca Tourism Office: +593 7-281-7060, [Official Website](http://www.cuenca.com.ec/)

- **Hidden Gems:** Explore the El Cajas National Park nearby for stunning landscapes.

4. Guayaquil:

- **History:** Founded in 1538, Guayaquil has evolved from a small fishing village to Ecuador's largest city and main port. Its strategic location made it a key player in trade and commerce, leading to rapid growth and urban development. Guayaquil has undergone significant transformations, becoming an economic powerhouse while maintaining its cultural identity.
-   **Key Attractions:** Malecon 2000, Las Peñas neighborhood, and Parque Seminario (Iguana Park).
- **When to Visit:** Year-round, but July to December offers more pleasant weather.
- **Contact Info:** Guayaquil Tourism Office: +593 4-259-0800, [Official Website](http://www.guayaquil.com.ec/)
-   **Culinary Delights:** Indulge in the local favorite, encebollado (fish soup).

5. Otavalo:

- **History:** Otavalo, known for its indigenous market, has a history dating back to pre-Incan times. The Otavaleños, skilled artisans, have maintained their traditions, creating a vibrant cultural atmosphere. The town played a role in the resistance against Spanish colonization, and today, it stands as a testament to Ecuador's indigenous heritage.
- **Key Attractions:** Otavalo Market, Peguche Waterfall, and Cuicocha Lake.
- **When to Visit:** Saturday is market day, but the town is lively throughout the week.
- **Contact Info:** Otavalo Tourism Office: +593 6-292-3737, [Official Website](http://www.otavalo.com.ec/)
- **Hidden Gems**: Visit the nearby village of Cotacachi for its leather goods.

6. Latacunga:

- **History:** Founded in 1534, Latacunga has a rich colonial history shaped by Spanish influence. The city has experienced periods of prosperity and challenges, with historical events such as the Mama Negra Festival symbolizing the fusion of indigenous and colonial traditions.
- **Key Attractions:** La Virgen de Agua Santa Cathedral, Cotopaxi Province, and the Mama Negra Festival.
- **When to Visit:** August for the vibrant Mama Negra Festival.
- **Contact Info:** Latacunga Tourism Office: +593 3-281-9055
- **Culinary Delights:** Try the traditional dish chugchucaras.

7. Cotopaxi National Park:

- **History:** Established in 1975, Cotopaxi National Park surrounds the towering Cotopaxi volcano. This active stratovolcano is an integral part of Ecuador's geological history, shaping the Andean landscape. The park is a haven for diverse flora and fauna, contributing to the country's commitment to environmental conservation.

- **Key Attractions:** Cotopaxi Volcano, Limpiopungo Lake, and the Cotopaxi Refuge.

- **When to Visit**: June to September for clearer skies and better visibility.

- **Contact Info:** Cotopaxi National Park Office: +593 2-252-7500, [Official Website](http://www.ambiente.gob.ec/parque-nacional-cotopaxi/)

- **Hidden Gems**: Explore the Pucará del Salitre archaeological site.

8. Tena:

- **History:** Tena, the capital of the Napo Province, carries a rich indigenous history. The town's location in the Amazon rainforest has played a role in its cultural and economic significance. Tena serves as a gateway for exploring the biodiversity of the Amazon basin, contributing to Ecuador's reputation as one of the world's most biodiverse countries.

- **Key Attractions:** Amazon Rainforest, Jatun Sacha Biological Reserve, and Misahualli River.

- **When to Visit:** Year-round, but the dry season from December to March is ideal.

- **Contact Info:** Tena Tourism Office: +593 6-288-6014

- **Culinary Delights:** Try traditional Amazonian cuisine with freshwater fish.

9. Puerto López:

- **History:** Puerto López, a coastal town, has a history deeply intertwined with fishing traditions. Serving as a base for exploring Machalilla National Park, it has become a hotspot for ecotourism and marine life enthusiasts. The town's cultural identity is reflected in its vibrant festivals and connections to ancient archaeological sites.
   - **Key Attractions**: Los Frailes Beach, Isla de la Plata, and whale-watching tours.
   - **When to Visit:** June to September for whale-watching season.
   - **Contact Info:** Puerto López Tourism Office: +593 5-258-2082
   - **Hidden Gems:** Explore the nearby Agua Blanca community for archaeological sites.

10. Ibarra:

- **History:** Founded in 1606, Ibarra boasts colonial architecture and a rich cultural history. The city has witnessed changes from Spanish colonial rule to its role in Ecuador's struggle for independence. Ibarra's cultural heritage is celebrated through events like the Fiesta de la Chirimoya, showcasing its blend of indigenous and colonial influences.

- **Key Attractions:** La Basilica Church, Parque Pedro Moncayo, and Yahuarcocha Lake.

- **When to Visit:** September for the Fiesta de la Chirimoya.

- **Contact Info:** Ibarra Tourism Office: +593 6-260-2988

- **Culinary Delights:** Taste the local favorite, helado de paila (handmade ice cream).

11. Salinas:

- **History:** Salinas, a popular beach resort, has a history rooted in its coastal location. Originally a small fishing village, it has transformed into a modern tourist destination. Salinas reflects Ecuador's evolution from traditional fishing practices to a thriving coastal economy.
  - **Key Attractions:** Salinas Beach, Chocolatera Point, and the Malecon.
  - **When to Visit:** December to April for beach activities.
  - **Contact Info:** Salinas Tourism Office: +593 4-277-8816
  - **Hidden Gems:** Explore the nearby El Paseo Shopping Center for local crafts.

12. Zaruma:

- **History:** Founded in 1593, Zaruma has a historical legacy shaped by its status as a mining town. The extraction of gold and silver brought prosperity and attracted settlers. Today, Zaruma's well-preserved architecture, including the Church of San Antonio de Padua, serves as a reminder of its mining heritage. The town continues to showcase its unique cultural identity through local traditions and festivals.

- **Key Attractions**: El Sexmo Mine, Church of San Antonio de Padua, and the Calle Larga viewpoint.

- **When to Visit:** The dry season from June to September.

- **Contact Info**: Zaruma Tourism Office: +593 7-270-9011

- **Culinary Delights:** Try the traditional Ecuadorian dish, cuy (guinea pig).

Currency:
Ecuador utilizes the US Dollar (USD) as its official currency, providing travelers with a familiar and widely accepted monetary system. ATMs are conveniently available in major cities and towns, ensuring easy access to cash. Credit cards are generally accepted in hotels, restaurants, and urban areas, offering flexibility in payment methods.

Language:
Spanish is the official language of Ecuador. While English is spoken in tourist hubs, especially by the younger population, learning a few basic Spanish phrases can enhance your interaction with locals and enrich your travel experience.

Visas:
Ecuador typically welcomes most travelers without requiring a visa for stays of up to 90 days. While European Union (EU) nationals often enjoy visa-free entry, it's crucial to check specific visa requirements, especially for non-Schengen countries, before embarking on your journey.

Money:
Ecuador boasts a widespread network of ATMs, ensuring convenient access to cash. These machines are available at airports, bus terminals, and throughout urban areas. Credit cards are widely accepted, providing secure and efficient payment options in major hotels and restaurants.

Mobile Phones:
Most international mobile phones, especially those from Europe and Australia, function seamlessly in Ecuador. Travelers from other regions should ensure their devices are set to roaming mode. For cost-effective local

communication, consider purchasing a local SIM card upon arrival.

Time:

Ecuador operates on Ecuador Time (ECT), which is equivalent to GMT/UTC minus 5 hours. Being aware of the time difference is essential for scheduling activities and making travel arrangements.

Room Tax:

Be mindful of the potential 'room occupancy tax' applicable in some accommodations, ranging from $1 to $5 per night. Specific details can be obtained from local lodgings or official websites.

Seasons:

Ecuador experiences diverse climatic seasons, each offering unique advantages:

- *High Season (Jun–Sep):* Ideal for exploring the Amazon rainforest and the Galápagos Islands. Expect increased prices and potential crowds.

- *Shoulder Season (Oct–Dec & Mar–May):* Enjoy pleasant weather and fewer crowds. Coastal regions experience a mix of sun and occasional rain.

- *Low Season (Jan–Feb)*: Coastal areas are warm, while the highlands may experience occasional showers. An excellent time for budget-conscious travelers.

Emergency Numbers:

In case of emergencies, be aware of the following contact numbers in Ecuador:

- Ambulance: 911
- Police: 911
- Fire: 911

When dialing from outside Ecuador, use your international access code followed by Ecuador's country code (593) and then the emergency number.

Useful Websites:

Make the most of your time in Ecuador with these online resources:
- *Ecuador Tourism Board:* [Official Website](http://www.ecuador.travel/)
- *Tren Ecuador*: [Official Website](http://www.trenecuador.com/)
- *Haciendas of Ecuador*: [Official Website](http://www.haciendas.org/)
- *Slow Food Ecuador:* [Official Website](http://www.slowfood.ec/)

Daily Costs:
Tailor your budget with these estimated daily costs:
- *Budget (Less than $50):* Hostel dorms range from $10 to $25, and affordable meals can be found for $5 to $10.
- *Midrange ($50–$150)*: Midrange hotels offer double rooms for $50 to $120. Dining at local restaurants costs approximately $15 to $30 per meal.
- *Top End (More than $150)*: Luxury experiences come with double rooms in upscale hotels ranging from $120 to $300. Fine dining may cost $30 to $100 per person.

Opening Hours:
Ecuador's opening hours vary by season, with high-season schedules generally from April to September and low-season hours from October or November to March. Keep in mind that opening hours may decrease during shoulder and low seasons. Common opening hours include:
- *Banks:* 9am–1pm and 3pm–7pm, Monday to Friday
- *Restaurants*: Noon–3pm and 6pm–10pm
- *Cafes:* 7am–8pm
- *Bars and clubs:* 9pm–2am
- *Shops:* 9am–6pm, Monday to Saturday

Arriving in Ecuador:
Depending on your arrival airport, transportation options to city centers include:

- Mariscal Sucre International Airport (Quito): Taxi fares range from $25 to $40, taking approximately 45 minutes.

- *José Joaquín de Olmedo International Airport (Guayaquil):* Taxis charge around $5 to $10, with a travel time of 10 to 15 minutes.

Armed with this practical information, you're ready to explore the wonders of Ecuador, embracing its diverse landscapes, rich culture, and warm hospitality.

What to Wear:

Ecuador, with its diverse climates and landscapes, demands versatile wardrobe choices. In the capital, Quito, where the weather is often cool and unpredictable, layers are essential. Coastal cities like Guayaquil experience warmer temperatures, making lightweight clothing, hats, and sunscreen crucial. In the Amazon rainforest, breathable and long-sleeved clothing protects against insects. For trekking in the Andes, sturdy hiking boots, waterproof jackets, and thermal layers are advisable. Remember to respect local customs when visiting indigenous communities by dressing modestly.

Sleeping:

Accommodations in Ecuador cater to various preferences and budgets:
- **Hotels:** Ranging from luxury establishments to budget-friendly options, hotels offer comfort and convenience.
- **Ecolodges:** Embrace Ecuador's natural beauty by staying in eco-friendly lodges, especially in the Amazon and Galápagos.
- **Hostels:** Ideal for budget-conscious travelers, hostels provide communal atmospheres and shared accommodations.
- **Haciendas**: Experience traditional Ecuadorian hospitality in historic haciendas, often located in the scenic highlands.

Prepare for Ecuador's diverse terrains with these essentials:
- **Hiking Gear**: If exploring the Andes or rainforest, sturdy hiking boots, a daypack, and moisture-wicking clothing are essential.
- **Insect Repellent:** Especially important for jungle excursions to protect against mosquitoes and other insects.
- **Rain Gear:** Given the varied climates, pack a waterproof jacket or poncho.
- **Electrical Adapter:** Ensure your devices stay charged with the correct adapter for Ecuador's outlets.
- **Spanish Phrasebook:** While some areas may have English speakers, having basic Spanish phrases enhances your experience and interactions.

Money:

Ecuador predominantly uses the US Dollar (USD). Credit and debit cards are widely accepted in urban areas, but it's advisable to carry cash when venturing into rural or remote regions. ATMs are accessible, but transaction fees may apply, so it's prudent to withdraw larger amounts at once.

Bargaining:
While bargaining is acceptable in markets, it's less common in formal stores. In indigenous markets, negotiating prices for crafts or souvenirs is often expected and can be a cultural experience.

Tipping:
Tipping practices in Ecuador vary:
- *Restaurants:* A service charge is sometimes included, but an additional tip of 5-10% is appreciated.

- Taxis: Rounding up the fare is customary.
- Guides and Drivers: For tours, a tip of $5-$10 per person per day is customary.

Respect Ecuador's cultural norms with these etiquette tips:
- **Greetings:** A handshake is customary, and a verbal greeting like "buenos días" (good morning) or "buenas tardes" (good afternoon) is polite. Cheek kissing is common among friends.
- **Asking for Help:** Use "permiso" (excuse me) to navigate crowded areas, and "por favor" (please) when requesting assistance.
- **Religious Sites**: When visiting churches or religious sites, dress modestly by covering shoulders and knees. Respect local customs and traditions.
These insights will help you navigate your first visit to Ecuador confidently, ensuring a rich and culturally immersive experience in this stunningly diverse country.

Andean Expedition - 2 Weeks

Embark on a thrilling exploration of Ecuador's Andean wonders.

Day 1 - 3: Quito

Commence your journey in the vibrant capital, Quito. Spend three days absorbing the rich culture and history, from the colonial Old Town to the panoramic views from the Teleferico. Delight in the bustling Otavalo Market and savor local Andean cuisine.

Day 4 - 6: Cotopaxi National Park

Venture to the majestic Cotopaxi National Park, home to the iconic Cotopaxi volcano. Immerse yourself in the high-altitude landscapes, hike to Limpiopungo Lagoon, and witness unique Andean wildlife.

Day 7 - 9: Baños

Explore the adventurous town of Baños, nestled at the base of the Tungurahua volcano. Engage in thrilling activities like zip-lining, cycling along the "Ruta de las Cascadas," and soaking in the rejuvenating thermal baths.

Day 10 - 12: Cuenca

Head to the UNESCO World Heritage city of Cuenca, renowned for its colonial architecture. Wander through cobbled streets, visit the impressive Cuenca Cathedral, and explore the vibrant local markets.

Day 13 - 15: Vilcabamba

Conclude your Andean expedition in Vilcabamba, known as the "Valley of Longevity." Enjoy the serene landscapes, partake in hiking or horseback riding, and embrace the tranquil atmosphere.

Embark on an immersive journey through the heart of the Amazon rainforest.

Day 1 - 3: Coca

Commence your adventure in Coca, the gateway to the Amazon. Board a canoe along the Napo River and arrive at a secluded eco-lodge deep in the jungle. Explore the rainforest's biodiversity and engage with indigenous communities.

Day 4 - 6: Yasuní National Park

Navigate to Yasuní National Park, one of the most biologically diverse areas on the planet. Encounter rare wildlife, from colorful birds to elusive jungle cats. Connect with local guides to learn about traditional Amazonian cultures.

Day 7 - 9: Tena

Journey to Tena, a hub for Amazonian adventures. Engage in thrilling activities like white-water rafting, jungle hikes, and canopy tours. Experience the unique flora and fauna that make the Amazon a global treasure.

Day 10 - 12: Misahuallí

Explore the charming town of Misahuallí, situated on the banks of the Napo River. Discover the local Kichwa culture, embark on a river excursion, and witness the beauty of the Amazonian sunset.

Day 13 - 15: Papallacta

Conclude your rainforest journey in Papallacta, known for its rejuvenating hot springs. Relax in the midst of nature, surrounded by cloud forests and hummingbirds, providing a perfect ending to your Amazonian exploration.

Discover the beauty and diversity of Ecuador's coastal regions.

Day 1 - 3: Guayaquil

Begin your coastal adventure in Guayaquil, Ecuador's largest city. Explore the historic Malecón 2000, visit the vibrant Las Peñas neighborhood, and savor local seafood delights.

Day 4 - 6: Montañita

Head to the bohemian beach town of Montañita. Embrace the laid-back atmosphere, ride the Pacific waves, and experience the town's eclectic nightlife. Explore nearby Isla de la Plata for a taste of the Galápagos without the crowds.

Day 7 - 9: Puerto López

Venture to Puerto López, a fishing village known for its stunning coastline. Embark on a whale-watching tour, explore Machalilla National Park, and relax on the pristine beaches.

Day 10 - 12: Cajas National Park

Experience the mystical cloud forests of Cajas National Park. Hike through the breathtaking landscapes, dotted with crystal-clear lakes and unique Andean flora. Discover the cultural richness of the local communities.

Day 13 - 15: Salinas

Conclude your coastal journey in Salinas, Ecuador's premier beach resort. Enjoy water sports, unwind on golden sands, and relish the fresh seafood at the Malecón. Bask in the sun as you reflect on the diverse coastal wonders.

These tailored itineraries offer a glimpse into the diverse landscapes, cultures, and adventures awaiting travelers in Ecuador. Whether exploring the Andes, the Amazon rainforest, or the coastal regions, each journey promises a unique and unforgettable experience.

The Culinary Calendar of Ecuador

In Ecuador, every season unfolds a unique culinary experience, offering a diverse array of flavors that captivate the senses throughout the year. Explore the country's gastronomic delights with this overview of the Ecuadorian culinary calendar:

Andean Harvest (March - May)

As spring arrives in the Andean region, Ecuador celebrates a bounty of fresh produce. Quinoa, potatoes, and various grains take center stage. This season coincides with traditional festivals like Inti Raymi, where locals showcase their agricultural prowess and indulge in vibrant, locally sourced dishes.

Coastal Bounty (June - August)

The coastal region of Ecuador comes alive with an abundance of seafood during the summer months. Delight in the catch of the day, including shrimp, ceviche, and a variety of fish dishes. Join the festivities of the Fiestas de Guayaquil, featuring coastal culinary delights and lively celebrations.

Amazonian Harvest (September - November)

Autumn in the Amazon rainforest introduces an array of exotic fruits, such as guava, passion fruit, and soursop. Indigenous communities celebrate the harvest with vibrant ceremonies, showcasing the region's rich culinary heritage. Explore traditional Amazonian dishes and savor the unique flavors of the jungle.

Highland Festivities (December - February)

As winter unfolds in the Ecuadorian highlands, the culinary scene is marked by festive treats. Indulge in traditional Andean dishes like locro de papa (potato soup) and llapingachos (stuffed potato patties). Join in the festivities of Inti Raymi in the highland villages, where locals share their culinary traditions.

Budget-Friendly Ecuadorian Delights

1. Llapingachos: Crispy potato patties filled with cheese, a staple in highland cuisine.

2. Ceviche de Camarón: Coastal Ecuador's flavorful shrimp ceviche, marinated in citrus juices and spices.

3. Empanadas de Viento: Airy, cheese-filled pastries that are a popular street food snack.

4. Encebollado: A hearty fish soup featuring yuca, tomatoes, and pickled red onions.

5. Bolon de Verde: Fried green plantain balls stuffed with cheese or meat, a tasty and filling option.

6. Choclo con Queso: Grilled corn on the cob served with fresh cheese, a beloved street food item.

1. Cuy (Guinea Pig): A traditional delicacy, often roasted or fried, particularly celebrated during festivals.

2. Seco de Chivo: Slow-cooked goat stew, infused with Ecuadorian spices and served with rice.

3. Caldo de Pata: A hearty soup made from cow's hoof, a unique and flavorful Andean dish.

4. Maito: Fish or meat wrapped in banana leaves and grilled, a traditional preparation in the Amazon.

5. Hormigas Culonas: Amazonian delicacy featuring large, roasted ants, offering a unique crunchy texture.

Regional Culinary Gems of Ecuador

Highlands:

Explore the culinary treasures of the highlands, where dishes like hornado (roast pork), llapingachos, and quimbolitos (sweet corn cakes) showcase the rich flavors of Andean cuisine. Don't miss the opportunity to indulge in the exquisite chocolates of Quito.

Coast:

Savor the coastal delights with dishes like encocado de camarones (shrimp in coconut sauce), ceviche de concha (shellfish ceviche), and the popular street food, viche de pescado (fish soup). Guayaquil, known as the "Pearl of the Pacific," offers a vibrant food scene with influences from Afro-Ecuadorian and indigenous cultures.

Amazon:

Immerse yourself in the Amazon's culinary diversity, featuring exotic fruits, freshwater fish, and dishes like tacacho con cecina (mashed plantains with pork). Experience the unique flavors of chicha, a fermented beverage made from yuca or maize.

Galápagos Islands:

Discover the gastronomic delights of the Galápagos Islands, where seafood takes center stage. Indulge in dishes like encocado de pescado (fish in coconut sauce) and langostinos al ajillo (garlic prawns). The islands offer a unique fusion of local and international flavors.

How to Eat & Drink Like an Ecuadorian?

To truly embrace Ecuadorian culture through its cuisine, follow these tips for an authentic dining experience:

Time of Eating:

- **Desayuno (Breakfast):** Start your day with a hearty breakfast, including local fruits, tigrillo (mashed green plantains), and bolón de verde (fried plantain balls).
- **Almuerzo (Lunch):** Enjoy the main meal of the day around noon, featuring traditional dishes like seco de pollo (chicken stew) or encebollado.
- **Merienda:** Take a mid-afternoon break with a cup of Ecuadorian coffee and a snack like humitas (steamed corn cakes).
- **Cena (Dinner):** Wind down your day with a lighter dinner, perhaps savoring a traditional locro de papa or a ceviche de pescado.

Buen provecho! Explore the diverse and flavorful world of Ecuadorian cuisine, where each region tells its unique culinary story.

Ecuador, a treasure trove of geographical wonders, beckons adventure enthusiasts to explore its diverse and thrilling landscapes. From the towering peaks of the Andes to the lush expanses of the Amazon rainforest and the pristine shores of the Pacific coastline, Ecuador offers an array of adrenaline-pumping activities. In this section, we will take a more in-depth look at the best adventure experiences that await thrill-seekers across the Ecuadorian terrain.

Hiking in Ecuador's Diverse Landscapes

Ecuador's varied topography unfolds numerous hiking opportunities for enthusiasts.
- **Mindo's Cloud Forest Trails:** Journey through the lush cloud forests of Mindo, discovering diverse flora and fauna. The well-maintained trails offer a perfect introduction to Ecuador's biodiversity.
- **Quilotoa Loop:** Trek the iconic Quilotoa Loop, a trail that encompasses the stunning Quilotoa crater lake. The loop takes you through indigenous villages, providing a cultural and scenic immersion.
- **Cajas National Park:** Explore the enchanting trails of Cajas National Park, navigating through a landscape of high-altitude lakes and moorlands. The park offers challenging routes for seasoned hikers.

- Amazon Rainforest Treks: Delve into the heart of the Amazon Rainforest for a unique jungle trekking experience. Encounter diverse wildlife and immerse yourself in the rich biodiversity of the region.

Cycling Adventures Through Ecuador's Scenic Routes

Cycling aficionados can explore Ecuador's picturesque landscapes through various routes:

- **Avenue of the Volcanoes:** Ride through the vibrant landscapes of the Avenue of the Volcanoes, surrounded by towering peaks. This route provides a unique perspective on Ecuador's geological wonders.

- **Andean Villages of the Sierra:** Pedal through the charming villages of the Sierra, immersing yourself in the cultural tapestry of the Andean highlands. The journey unveils the daily life of indigenous communities.

- **Coastal Cycling near Puerto Lopez:** Explore coastal routes near Puerto Lopez, cycling along the Pacific shores. The combination of sea breezes and scenic views adds an extra dimension to your cycling adventure.

- Challenging Climbs of the Andes: For those seeking more challenging climbs, tackle the ascents of the Andes, including routes near Cotopaxi and Chimborazo. These rides offer both a physical and visual feast.

Skiing in the Andean Highlands

Ecuador's Andean highlands provide a unique skiing experience against the backdrop of volcanic landscapes:
- **Antisana and Cayambe Resorts:** Visit the ski resorts of Antisana and Cayambe for a one-of-a-kind skiing adventure. Skiing enthusiasts can carve through the snow with the Andean peaks as their backdrop.

Diving into Ecuador's Marine Wonders

Ecuador's coastal waters and marine reserves offer a paradise for divers:
- **Galápagos Islands:** Explore the underwater wonders of the Galápagos Islands, encountering hammerhead sharks, sea lions, and marine iguanas. The Galápagos Marine Reserve is a UNESCO World Heritage site known for its unique marine biodiversity.

- **Machalilla Marine Reserve:** Dive into the vibrant coral reefs and diverse marine life off the coast of Puerto Lopez in the Machalilla Marine Reserve. This area is teeming with underwater treasures.

Whitewater Adventures in Ecuador's Rivers

Thrill-seekers can navigate Ecuador's rivers for an adrenaline-pumping whitewater experience:
- **Amazon Basin Rivers (Napo and Pastaza):** Experience challenging rapids surrounded by lush rainforest in the rivers of the Amazon Basin. The Napo and Pastaza rivers provide an exhilarating whitewater adventure.
- **Tena Region**: Tena is a hub for rafting and kayaking enthusiasts, offering thrilling experiences in the heart of Ecuador's diverse waterways.

Ecuador's diverse landscapes offer rock climbing opportunities for adventurers:
- **Baños Valley:** The lush valleys of Baños provide challenging climbs with stunning waterfall views. Rock climbing here is a perfect combination of adventure and breathtaking scenery.
- **Granite Walls of Cajas National Park:** Explore the granite walls of Cajas National Park for a unique rock climbing experience. The park offers routes suitable for climbers of varying skill levels.

Sailing Ecuador's Pacific Coast and Galápagos Islands

Ecuador's Pacific coastline and the Galápagos Islands invite sailing enthusiasts to explore their pristine waters:
- **Isla de la Plata:** Charter a yacht to navigate the secluded bays of Isla de la Plata, known as the "Poor Man's Galápagos." The island offers a quieter but equally stunning sailing experience.
- **Galápagos Archipelago:** Embark on a sailing adventure around the Galápagos archipelago, discovering the unique landscapes and wildlife of this UNESCO World Heritage site.

Windsurfing in Ecuador's Coastal Paradises

Ecuador's Pacific coast, especially spots like Manta and Canoa, offers excellent conditions for windsurfing:
- **Manta and Canoa:** Enjoy the thrill of windsurfing against the backdrop of the Pacific breeze. These coastal paradises provide ideal conditions for both beginners and experienced windsurfers.

Best Times to Experience Adventure in Ecuador

- **June to September:** Ideal for cycling adventures and skiing in the Andean highlands.
- **December to February:** Perfect for rock climbing and exploring diverse landscapes.
- **April to August:** Optimal for whitewater adventures and diving into the marine wonders.
- **Year-round:** Hiking enthusiasts can explore Ecuador's diverse trails throughout the year.

Ecuador's breathtaking landscapes, ranging from the Andes to the Amazon and the Pacific, create an adventure playground for those seeking thrilling experiences. Whether you're drawn to the mountains, rivers, or the ocean, Ecuador promises unforgettable moments for the adventurous traveler.

Pre-Columbian Ecuador - The Indigenous Cultures

Ecuador's history dates back to ancient times when various indigenous cultures inhabited its diverse landscapes. The region that is now Ecuador was home to several advanced civilizations, each contributing to the rich tapestry of pre-Columbian history.

1. Valdivia Culture (3500–1800 BCE):

One of the earliest known cultures in the region, the Valdivia people, settled along the coastal areas. They were skilled potters and agriculturists, leaving behind artifacts and evidence of early agricultural practices.

2. Chorrera Culture (1800–300 BCE):

Following the Valdivia culture, the Chorrera people emerged, emphasizing ceremonial centers and complex societies. They made significant advancements in pottery, showcasing intricate designs and cultural symbolism.

3. Machalilla Culture (2000 BCE – 800 CE):

The Machalilla people, along the coast, are recognized for their intricate ceramics and trade networks. Their influence extended into the highlands, contributing to the cultural diversity of ancient Ecuador.

4. Manteño-Huancavilca Culture (800–1534 CE):

The Manteño-Huancavilca culture flourished on the coast, engaging in maritime trade and establishing port cities. They were skilled sailors and traders, interacting with other Andean cultures.

5. Quitu-Cara Confederation (Pre-15th Century):

In the Sierra region, the Quitu and Cara tribes formed a confederation, establishing the basis for what would later become the capital city of Quito. Their agricultural practices and social structures laid the foundation for the region's highland civilizations.

The Inca Empire, renowned for its vast Andean domain, extended its influence into present-day Ecuador during the 15th century. This era marked a period of integration and conquest as the Inca civilization absorbed the diverse cultures of the region.

1. Inca Expansion into Ecuador:
Under the rule of Emperor Huayna Capac, the Inca Empire expanded its reach northward, incorporating parts of what is now Ecuador into its vast territory. The Inca introduced their administrative and agricultural practices, leaving a lasting impact on the local populations.

2. Integration of Local Cultures:
Rather than imposing a complete cultural assimilation, the Inca Empire often integrated local cultures into their administrative and religious systems. This approach allowed for a degree of cultural diversity within the empire while maintaining a centralized governing structure.

3. Quito as an Inca Center:
The city of Quito, founded by the Quitu-Cara tribes, became an important Inca center. The Incas recognized its strategic significance, transforming it into a regional administrative and religious hub. The Temple of the Sun (Quito's current-day La Basilica) and other structures reflected the Inca influence.

4. Impact on Agriculture and Architecture:
The Inca Empire introduced advanced agricultural techniques, such as terrace farming, to optimize food production in the challenging Andean terrain. Additionally, their architectural expertise is evident in structures like Ingapirca, a significant Inca archaeological site in Ecuador.

The arrival of Spanish conquistadors in the early 16th century marked a pivotal moment in Ecuador's history, leading to significant cultural, social, and political changes. This period of conquest and colonization had lasting impacts on the indigenous civilizations that had thrived for centuries.

1. Francisco Pizarro and the Conquest of the Inca Empire:

In 1532, Spanish conquistador Francisco Pizarro, lured by tales of Inca wealth, arrived in the Andean region. The Inca Empire was already weakened by internal strife and diseases introduced by earlier Spanish expeditions. Pizarro exploited these vulnerabilities, capturing the Inca emperor Atahualpa and ultimately leading to the fall of the Inca Empire.

2. Spanish Colonization and Cultural Assimilation:

With the Inca Empire subdued, the Spanish Crown claimed control over the newly acquired territories, including present-day Ecuador. The Spanish imposed their language, religion, and governance systems, initiating a process of cultural assimilation that significantly transformed the indigenous way of life.

3. Encomienda System and Labor Exploitation:

The encomienda system, established by the Spanish Crown, granted land and indigenous labor to Spanish colonizers. This system, purportedly designed to protect and convert the indigenous populations, often led to exploitation and abuse. Indigenous communities faced forced labor, cultural suppression, and the introduction of new diseases that decimated their numbers.

4. Establishment of Quito as a Colonial Center:

Quito, strategically located in the Andean highlands, became a key colonial center. The Spanish colonial authorities constructed churches, administrative buildings, and mansions, shaping the city's colonial architecture. The historic center of Quito, with its well-preserved colonial structures, is now a UNESCO World Heritage Site.

The 19th century brought profound changes to Ecuador as it embarked on the tumultuous journey to independence from Spanish rule. Subsequently, the young nation faced numerous challenges, including political instability, border disputes, and economic struggles. The 20th century witnessed further transformations, both politically and socially, shaping Ecuador into the diverse and vibrant country it is today.

1. Struggle for Independence (1809-1822):

Ecuador actively participated in the broader South American struggle for independence from Spanish rule. The seeds of rebellion were sown in 1809 when Quito initiated the fight for independence. However, achieving full sovereignty took over a decade of conflicts, battles, and shifting alliances. The decisive Battle of Pichincha in 1822, led by leaders such as Antonio José de Sucre and Simón Bolívar, secured Ecuador's independence.

2. The Gran Colombia Experiment:

Following independence, Ecuador briefly joined the union of Gran Colombia, a political entity comprising modern-day Colombia, Venezuela, Ecuador, and Panama, under the leadership of Simón Bolívar. Internal disagreements and regional tensions, however, led to the dissolution of Gran Colombia in 1830, allowing Ecuador to emerge as an independent republic.

3. Territorial Challenges and Border Disputes:

Throughout the 19th and early 20th centuries, Ecuador grappled with territorial challenges and border disputes.

The most significant of these was the long-standing dispute with Peru over the Amazonian territories. The signing of the Rio Protocol in 1942, mediated by the United States, brought a temporary resolution to the conflict.

4. Economic Struggles and Political Instability:

Ecuador faced economic challenges throughout the 19th and early 20th centuries, primarily due to its dependence on a few export commodities. The global economic downturns, coupled with political instability and frequent changes in leadership, hindered the country's development. The discovery of oil in the Amazon in the 20th century, while bringing economic opportunities, also fueled environmental concerns and social tensions.

5. Late 20th Century and Beyond:

The latter half of the 20th century witnessed efforts to modernize Ecuador's economy and address social inequalities. Constitutional reforms, agrarian reforms, and attempts to diversify the economy were implemented. However, political instability persisted, marked by a series of coups and changes in government.

6. Indigenous Rights and Social Movements:

A notable development in late 20th-century Ecuador was the rise of indigenous movements advocating for land rights, cultural recognition, and political representation. The indigenous movement played a crucial role in shaping Ecuador's modern identity, contributing to the drafting of a more inclusive constitution in 1998.

7. 21st Century Challenges and Achievements:

The 21st century brought both challenges and achievements for Ecuador. Economic fluctuations, natural disasters, and political controversies have marked the country's recent history. Additionally, efforts to balance economic development with environmental conservation, especially in the Amazon rainforest, have become central to the national discourse.

In conclusion, Ecuador's history is a tapestry woven with threads of struggle, resilience, and transformation. From the ancient civilizations of the Andes to the challenges of the modern era, Ecuador has navigated a complex journey, leaving an indelible mark on its cultural, political, and social landscape.

Accommodation Options in Ecuador

Ecuador, a land of diverse landscapes and rich cultural heritage, offers a wide range of accommodation options for travelers. Whether you seek the quaint charm of rural settings, the comfort of urban retreats, or unique experiences in unconventional lodgings, Ecuador has it all. Here's an in-depth guide to help you navigate the varied landscape of accommodations in this South American gem.

1. Booking in Advance:

Ecuador experiences peak tourist seasons, especially during festivals and holidays. Booking in advance is advisable, particularly for popular destinations like the Galápagos Islands or during events like the Inti Raymi festival. Secure your accommodations early to ensure availability, especially in high-demand periods.

2. Seasonal Price Dynamics:

Understanding Ecuador's climate and tourist seasons is crucial for budget planning. High tourist seasons coincide with the dry months (June to September), attracting visitors to the Amazon, the Andes, and the Galápagos. Prices may spike during these periods, making it prudent to explore the shoulder seasons for more budget-friendly options.

3. Geographical Price Variations:

Accommodation costs in Ecuador can vary significantly by location. While the Galápagos Islands and Quito might command higher prices, charming towns in the Andean highlands or the Amazon basin can offer more budget-friendly choices. Factor in regional price variations when crafting your travel itinerary.

For a truly immersive experience, consider staying in indigenous communities. Community-based tourism initiatives offer a chance to engage with local traditions and lifestyles. Options range from homestays to community-run lodges, providing an authentic and enriching experience.

Price Range: $20 - $60 per night

Exploring the Amazon rainforest warrants a stay in one of its unique jungle lodges. These lodges offer a blend of comfort and proximity to nature. Consider lodges in Yasuní National Park or Cuyabeno Wildlife Reserve, each providing a distinctive Amazonian experience.

Price Range: $80 - $250 per night

Ecuador's Pacific coastline beckons beach lovers, and the options for coastal accommodations are diverse. From upscale beach resorts to eco-friendly beachfront cabins, you can find the perfect stay to enjoy the sun, sea, and vibrant coastal culture.

Price Range: $50 - $200 per night

Ecuador boasts a plethora of historic haciendas, each with its unique charm. These former colonial estates have been converted into luxurious accommodations, offering a glimpse into Ecuador's aristocratic past. Immerse yourself in the country's history while enjoying modern comforts.

Price Range: $100 - $300 per night

Backpackers and budget-conscious travelers can explore Ecuador's network of hostels. These range from vibrant

and social spaces to quiet retreats, often nestled in the heart of cities or amid scenic landscapes. Hostels provide an excellent opportunity to connect with fellow travelers.
Price Range: $10 - $30 per night

9. Ecolodges in the Cloud Forest:

The cloud forests of Ecuador offer a mystical setting for nature enthusiasts. Ecolodges, blending seamlessly with the lush surroundings, provide a sustainable and immersive stay. Mindo and Mindo-Nambillo Cloud Forest Reserves are popular locations for these unique accommodations.
Price Range: $60 - $150 per night

10. Rural Cottages in the Andean Highlands:

Experience the tranquility of the Andean highlands by staying in rural cottages. These cozy accommodations, often run by local families, offer an escape into nature. Wake up to stunning mountain views and enjoy the warmth of Ecuadorian hospitality.
Price Range: $40 - $120 per night

11. City Boutique Hotels:

Quito, Cuenca, and Guayaquil boast boutique hotels that combine modern luxury with a touch of local flair. These urban retreats provide a comfortable stay amid the bustling energy of Ecuador's vibrant cities.
Price Range: $80 - $200 per night

12. Mountain Refuges for Trekkers:

For those exploring the Andean trails, mountain refuges are strategically located for trekking enthusiasts. Cotopaxi National Park and Quilotoa Loop have refuges that cater to hikers, providing a rustic yet essential shelter.
Price Range: $30 - $80 per night

13. Ecuadorian Amazon River Cruises:

Embark on a unique accommodation experience with Amazon river cruises. These floating lodges take you deep into the heart of the Amazon, offering a blend of comfort and adventure. Explore the waterways and encounter incredible biodiversity.

Price Range: $200 - $500 per night

14. Eco-Friendly Treehouse Stays:

For an unforgettable experience, consider eco-friendly treehouse stays in the jungle regions. These sustainable accommodations allow you to connect with nature while minimizing your environmental impact.

Price Range: $80 - $200 per night

15. All-Inclusive Rainforest Resorts:

The Amazon and its tributaries are home to all-inclusive rainforest resorts. These luxury accommodations offer a comprehensive experience, including guided excursions, wildlife spotting, and cultural interactions with local communities.

Price Range: $300 - $800 per night

16. Island Hopping in the Galápagos:

Galápagos Islands, a UNESCO World Heritage site, offer a range of accommodations for island hopping. From luxury resorts to budget-friendly guesthouses, tailor your stay to match the islands you plan to explore.

Price Range: $100 - $500 per night

17. Budget-Friendly Guesthouses:

Throughout Ecuador, you'll find budget-friendly guesthouses, often family-run, providing a cozy and intimate stay. These guesthouses offer personalized attention and a chance to connect with the local way of life.

Price Range: $20 - $50 per night

18. Rural Community Lodges in the Highlands:

Support sustainable tourism by staying in rural community lodges in the highlands. These lodges, managed by local communities, offer a genuine cultural experience while contributing to the preservation of indigenous traditions.

Price Range: $30 - $80 per night

19. Thermal Springs Retreats:

Ecuador's thermal springs, such as those in Baños, provide a rejuvenating retreat. Stay in lodges near these natural wonders, allowing you to indulge in the therapeutic benefits of the mineral-rich waters.

Price Range: $50 - $150 per night

20. Volunteer and Cultural Exchange Accommodations:

Engage in cultural exchange or volunteer programs, where accommodations are often provided. Immerse yourself in local communities, contribute to meaningful projects, and forge connections that go beyond conventional stays.

Price Range: Varies; often included in program fees

21. Luxury Resorts in the Cloud Forest:

Experience unparalleled luxury in cloud forest resorts. These high-end accommodations offer not only lavish amenities but also breathtaking views of the lush surroundings. Ideal for those seeking a premium retreat.

Price Range: $200 - $600 per night

22. Historic Center Boutique Hostels:

Stay in the heart of Ecuador's historic centers by choosing boutique hostels. These budget-friendly yet stylish accommodations provide easy access to cultural sites, museums, and the vibrant atmosphere of colonial cities.

Price Range: $30 - $80 per night

23. Family-Friendly Beach Resorts:

Ecuador's coastal regions feature family-friendly beach resorts. Enjoy a blend of relaxation and entertainment, with many resorts offering activities for both adults and children.

Price Range: $80 - $250 per night

24. Budget Accommodations in Indigenous Villages:

Connect with indigenous cultures by opting for budget accommodations in villages. Experience traditional lifestyles, participate in local customs, and contribute to community-based tourism initiatives.

Price Range: $20 - $60 per night

25. Historical District Bed and Breakfasts:

Explore Ecuador's historical districts by staying in bed and breakfasts. These charming lodgings, often situated in colonial-era buildings, provide an intimate and cozy atmosphere.

Price Range: $40 - $100 per night

26. Mountain Cabins for Hikers and Climbers:

Hikers and climbers can find refuge in mountain cabins strategically located near hiking and climbing trails. Whether in the Andes or the Sierra, these cabins offer a rustic yet comfortable retreat.

Price Range: $30 - $70 per night

27. Educational Farm Stays:

Families or those seeking an educational experience can opt for farm stays. Learn about sustainable agriculture, participate in daily farm activities, and enjoy the tranquility of rural settings.

Price Range: $20 - $60 per night

28. City Center Apart-Hotels:

Stay in the heart of Ecuadorian cities by choosing apart-hotels in city centers. These accommodations blend the convenience of hotel services with the independence of apartment living.

Price Range: $60 - $150 per night

29. Artistic Retreats in Coastal Towns:

Coastal towns like Montañita and Puerto López host artistic retreats, providing a haven for creative souls. Stay in unique lodgings that foster artistic expression while enjoying the coastal ambiance.

Price Range: $40 - $100 per night

Explore the depths of the rainforest by staying in wilderness camps. These eco-friendly camps offer an immersive experience, allowing you to witness the incredible biodiversity of the Amazon.

Price Range: $60 - $150 per night

In conclusion, Ecuador's accommodation options are as diverse as its landscapes. Whether you're a nature enthusiast, cultural explorer, or luxury seeker, Ecuador caters to every taste and preference. As you plan your Ecuadorian adventure, consider the multitude of accommodation choices that promise not just a place to stay but a unique and enriching experience.

Customs Regulations in Ecuador

When embarking on a journey to Ecuador, understanding the customs regulations and practical information is crucial for a smooth and enjoyable trip. Here's an in-depth overview of customs regulations, duty-free allowances, and essential details to enhance your travel experience:

Duty-Free Allowances for Visitors:

Ecuador, as a country with diverse landscapes and vibrant culture, has specific duty-free allowances for visitors arriving from non-Ecuadorian destinations. Travelers can import certain items duty-free, providing an opportunity for tax-free shopping. Here are the duty-free allowances:

- **Spirits and Wine:** Travelers are allowed to bring a limited quantity of spirits and wine. Typically, this allowance includes one liter of spirits or two liters of wine.

- **Perfume and Eau de Toilette**: Visitors can import a reasonable amount of perfume and eau de toilette for personal use. Common allowances include 50 grams of perfume and 250 milliliters of eau de toilette.
- **Tobacco Products:** Ecuador allows a specific quantity of tobacco products duty-free. This often includes 200 cigarettes. Exceeding these limits requires a declaration upon arrival, and appropriate duties must be paid.
- **Other Goods:** Visitors are permitted to bring other goods up to a specified total value without incurring duties. This limit typically ranges up to $500, encouraging travelers to explore local markets and crafts.

Any items surpassing these allowances should be declared upon entry, and the necessary duties must be paid. For high-value purchases, there may be opportunities for non-Ecuadorian citizens to reclaim value-added tax, offering savings on significant expenditures.

Discounts and Special Cards:

Ecuador offers various discount options for travelers, enriching the exploration experience:
- **Age-Based Discounts:** Visitors may enjoy age-based discounts at cultural sites and attractions. Typically, those under 18 and over 65 receive free or reduced admission. Additionally, individuals aged 18 to 25 often qualify for discounted rates, although eligibility might be limited to certain categories of visitors.
- **Special Discount Cards**: Some cities and regions in Ecuador provide special discount cards. These cards, offer benefits like free or reduced admission to museums and other attractions. Exploring biglietto cumulativo options allows visitors access to multiple sights at a lower combined cost.
- **International Youth Cards:** The International Youth Card extends discounts on hotels, museums, restaurants, and

more. Students, teachers, and youth cardholders can benefit from cost savings on various services. These cards are obtainable from youth travel agencies globally.

Navigating daily aspects of travel in Ecuador requires awareness of certain practical details:

- **Electricity:** Ecuador adheres to the standard South American electrical specifications of 120V with a frequency of 60Hz. Travelers should ensure they have the appropriate adapters for their electronic devices.
- **Power Outlets:** Ecuadorian power outlets generally accept plugs with two flat or round pins. It's advisable to carry suitable adapters to keep devices charged during your travels.

Embassies & Consulates:

Being aware of the locations and contacts for embassies and consulates is essential for travelers requiring assistance. Here are contacts for selected embassies and consulates in Ecuador:

- Australian Embassy/Consulate: Quito and Guayaquil
- Canadian Embassy/Consulate: Quito and Guayaquil
- French Embassy/Consulate: Quito and Cuenca
- German Embassy/Consulate: Quito and Guayaquil
- Japanese Embassy/Consulate: Quito and Guayaquil
- UK Embassy/Consulate: Quito and Cuenca
- US Embassy/Consulate: Quito and Guayaquil

These diplomatic missions serve as valuable resources for travelers, offering assistance and support when needed during their exploration of Ecuador.

Arming yourself with knowledge of customs regulations, discount opportunities, and practical information will undoubtedly enhance your travel experience in Ecuador. Whether delving into the diverse landscapes, vibrant cities, or cultural treasures, being well-informed ensures a seamless and enriching journey.

Money Matters in Ecuador

When embarking on a journey to Ecuador, understanding the local currency and mastering the practical aspects of managing your finances are essential. Here's a detailed guide to money matters in Ecuador:

Currency:

Ecuador uses the United States Dollar (USD) as its official currency. You'll encounter dollar bills and coins in various denominations, including $100, $50, $20, $10, $5, $2, and $1 bills, as well as 50, 25, 10, 5, and 1 cent coins. Make sure to carry a mix of bills and coins for convenience.

ATMs & Credit Cards:

- **ATMs (Cajeros Automáticos):** ATMs are widespread throughout Ecuador's urban and tourist areas, providing a convenient way to obtain local currency. Major international credit and debit cards are widely accepted at ATMs displaying corresponding logos.
- **Credit Cards:** Visa and MasterCard are generally accepted in urban centers, hotels, restaurants, and larger establishments. However, it's advisable to carry cash when venturing into more remote areas, markets, or smaller establishments where card acceptance may be limited.
- **Card Usage:** Credit and debit cards are suitable for most transactions. They can be used for hotel payments, restaurant bills, shopping, and even some transportation services.
- **Bank Charges:** Before using your cards abroad, check with your bank regarding foreign transaction fees. These fees usually range around 3%, and additional charges may

apply for ATM withdrawals. It's recommended to notify your bank of your travel dates to avoid any potential issues.

- Lost or Stolen Cards: In the unfortunate event of a lost or stolen card, contact your card issuer immediately to report it and prevent unauthorized use. Here are the contact numbers for major card issuers:

- Visa: Call at %800 847 2911
- MasterCard: Call at %800 307 7309
- American Express: Contact the number on the back of your card

Money Changers:

Currency exchange services can be found at banks, exchange offices, and even some hotels. While banks typically offer favorable rates, exchange offices may provide extended hours of service. Be aware of commissions and rates at exchange offices, ensuring you get the best value for your money.

Taxes & Refunds:

Ecuador has a value-added tax (VAT), known as IVA (Impuesto al Valor Agregado), which is included in the displayed prices. As a traveler, you won't be eligible for a VAT refund. Ensure your budget considers this tax when making purchases.

Tipping:

Tipping practices in Ecuador are generally modest compared to some Western countries. While not obligatory, tips for good service are appreciated. Here's a guideline:

- Restaurants: 5-10% is customary if a service charge is not included.

- Bars: Small change or rounding up is common.

- Hotels: Tipping for exceptional service, such as assistance with luggage or room service, is appreciated.

Post:

The Ecuadorian postal service is reliable, and you can purchase stamps at post offices and authorized vendors. Postage costs vary based on the weight, size, and destination of your mail. Opt for "correo prioritario" (priority mail) for faster delivery within Ecuador and internationally.

Understanding these financial aspects will empower you to navigate Ecuador's monetary landscape seamlessly, ensuring a financially sound and enjoyable travel experience.

Public Holidays in Ecuador

Understanding the public holidays in Ecuador is crucial for planning your visit, as they may impact various aspects of your travel experience. Here are some of the major public holidays observed in Ecuador:

- New Year's Day (Año Nuevo) - January 1: The beginning of the year is celebrated with various festivities and events.
- Carnival (Carnaval) - February/March: This vibrant and lively celebration, marking the beginning of Lent, involves parades, water fights, and street parties.
- Good Friday (Viernes Santo) - March/April: A significant religious holiday observed with processions and events.
- Labour Day (Día del Trabajo) - May 1: Commemorating workers' rights, this day may involve rallies and demonstrations.
- Battle of Pichincha (Batalla del Pichincha) - May 24: Honoring the Battle of Pichincha, a key event in Ecuador's fight for independence.
- Inti Raymi (Celebration of the Sun) - June 21: A traditional indigenous celebration of the sun, marking the solstice with cultural events.

- Independence Day (Día de la Independencia) - August 10: Celebrating Ecuador's independence from Spanish rule with patriotic events.
- Foundation of Guayaquil (Fundación de Guayaquil) - July 25: Guayaquil celebrates its founding with parades and cultural activities.
- Independence of Cuenca (Independencia de Cuenca) - November 3: Commemorating Cuenca's independence with parades and festivities.
- All Souls' Day (Día de los Difuntos) - November 2: Families visit cemeteries to honor and remember their deceased loved ones.
- Quito Foundation Day (Fundación de Quito) - December 6: Quito celebrates its foundation with various events and festivities.
- Christmas (Navidad) - December 25: Christmas is a widely celebrated holiday with festive decorations and family gatherings.

Holiday Travel Considerations:

It's essential to be aware that during holidays, especially Carnival and Christmas, many Ecuadorians travel, and popular tourist destinations may experience increased crowds. Plan your itinerary accordingly to make the most of your visit.

Telephone and Communication in Ecuador:

When it comes to staying connected in Ecuador, consider the following:
- **Domestic Calls:** Ecuador has a telephone area code system, and area codes are integral to telephone numbers. Familiarize yourself with the area codes when making domestic calls.

- **International Calls:** Utilize low-cost communication apps like WhatsApp and Skype for international calls. Internet cafes and call centers in major cities also offer affordable options.

- **Mobile Phones:** Ecuador operates on the GSM 850/1900 system. Ensure your mobile phone is compatible, or consider purchasing a local SIM card for your visit.

- **Payphones & Phone Cards:** Payphones are available, and phone cards can be purchased at various outlets. They come in different denominations and have expiration dates.

- **Time Zone:** Ecuador is in the Ecuador Time (ECT) zone, which is UTC-5. It does not observe daylight-saving time.

Understanding Ecuador's public holidays and communication landscape will contribute to a smooth and enjoyable travel experience.

Visas and Residency in Ecuador

When planning a visit to Ecuador, it's vital to understand the visa and residency regulations. Here's a comprehensive overview to guide travelers:

1. Tourist Entry Requirements:

 - Citizens from various countries, including the United States, Canada, Australia, the European Union, and many South American nations, can enter Ecuador for tourism purposes without a visa for stays of up to 90 days.

 - Ensure your passport is valid for at least six months beyond your planned departure date.

2. Visa Extensions for Tourists:

 - If you wish to extend your stay beyond the initial 90 days, you can apply for a visa extension at the Ministry of Foreign Affairs and Human Mobility in Ecuador.

3. Work and Study Visas:

- If you intend to work or study in Ecuador, you'll need to apply for the relevant visa before traveling.
- Work visas require a job offer from an Ecuadorian employer, while study visas necessitate acceptance into a recognized educational institution in Ecuador.

4. Residency for Foreign Nationals:
- Foreign nationals seeking permanent residency in Ecuador can apply through various pathways, including the investor's visa, pensioner's visa, or professional visa.
- Each category has specific requirements, such as demonstrating a stable income or making a qualifying investment in the country.

5. Visa Application Process:
- The visa application process may vary depending on the type of visa you are seeking.
- Generally, you'll need to submit a completed application form, passport-sized photos, a valid passport, and supporting documents relevant to your visa category.
- It's advisable to check with the nearest Ecuadorian embassy or consulate for the most up-to-date requirements.

6. Temporary Residency for Pensioners:
- Ecuador offers a popular visa option for retirees, allowing individuals with a stable pension to apply for temporary residency.

7. Cultural Exchange Visas:
- For individuals participating in cultural exchange programs, there are specific visa options. This includes artists, musicians, and professionals engaging in collaborative projects.

8. Proof of Funds and Accommodation:
- Some visa categories may require proof of financial means to support yourself during your stay.

- Having confirmed accommodation details, whether a hotel reservation or a rental agreement, is often a visa application requirement.

9. Visa Renewals:

- Visa renewals can usually be done within Ecuador by applying to the Ministry of Foreign Affairs and Human Mobility. Ensure you start the renewal process well before your current visa expires.

10. Always Verify Requirements:

- Visa and residency requirements can change, so it's crucial to verify the latest information with official sources or seek assistance from the nearest Ecuadorian embassy or consulate.

Understanding Ecuador's visa and residency landscape ensures a legal and hassle-free stay in this diverse and welcoming country. Always stay informed and plan accordingly to make the most of your time in Ecuador.

Traveling to Ecuador

Ecuador provides diverse transportation options, facilitating accessibility for travelers from various parts of the world. The country is well-connected by air, land, and sea, ensuring convenient access to desired destinations.

By Air:

Ecuador boasts several international airports, with Quito's Mariscal Sucre International Airport and Guayaquil's José Joaquín de Olmedo International Airport serving as primary entry points. Airlines such as TAME and international carriers like American Airlines, LATAM, and Avianca operate flights connecting Ecuador to major global hubs. Numerous intra-South American flights make travel within the continent accessible.

Entering the Country:

- Citizens of many countries, including the United States, Canada, and those within the European Union, can enter Ecuador for tourism without a visa for stays up to 90 days.
- Ensure your passport validity meets the requirements for your entire stay.
- Carry your passport at all times, as it's necessary for police registration, especially when checking into hotels.

By Land:

Ecuador's extensive land transportation network facilitates connections with neighboring countries. Key border crossings include:

- **Colombia:** Cross from Ipiales to Tulcán via Pan-American Highway (E35).
- **Peru**: Entry points include Aguas Verdes to Huaquillas via Pan-American Highway (E25) and La Tina to Macará via E682.

By Bus:

Buses provide a cost-effective means of travel, although they may be less frequent and comfortable than trains. Companies like Cruz del Sur and Ormeño offer international bus services connecting Ecuador to Peru and Colombia.

By Car and Motorcycle:

- International driving permits are advisable for road travel.
- Ensure your vehicle displays its nationality plate and carry proof of ownership and insurance.
- Ecuador's roads offer scenic routes suitable for motorcycle touring, with helmets and a motorcycle license being mandatory.

By Train:

While Ecuador does not have an extensive train network, it offers a unique experience with services like Tren Crucero, providing scenic journeys through the Andes.

Train travel within Ecuador may be limited, but it offers an eco-friendly option for shorter distances.

Ecuador's coastal location allows sea travel connections. While less common than air and land options, ferry services operate seasonally. Prices vary, and some routes may transport vehicles for an additional fee.

Travel Tips:

- Be aware of visa requirements and entry regulations.
- Research and plan for land border crossings, considering customs controls.
- Verify vehicle insurance and ownership documentation for road travel.
- Check ferry schedules and routes for sea travel.

Understanding Ecuador's transportation options ensures a smooth and enjoyable journey, allowing travelers to explore the diverse landscapes and cultures of this South American gem.

Getting Around Ecuador

Once you've landed in Ecuador, exploring the country becomes a seamless experience with its diverse transportation options, including buses, domestic flights, bicycles, boats, taxis, trains, cars, and motorcycles.

By Air:

For domestic flights within Ecuador, you can rely on airlines such as TAME and LATAM. Prices for domestic flights vary, with one-way tickets ranging from $50 to $150 or more, depending on the destination and time of booking.

By Bicycle:

Cycling is a popular and eco-friendly way to explore Ecuador. You can bring your own bicycle or rent one locally. Rental prices for bicycles range from $10 to $30 per day, with discounts for weekly or monthly rentals.

By Boat:
To reach islands like the Galápagos or coastal destinations, various ferry services are available. Prices for ferry tickets vary based on the route and type of service. For example, a passenger ferry to the Galápagos can cost between $30 and $70, while a ferry carrying a vehicle might range from $100 to $200.

By Bus and Metro:
Ecuadorian cities feature well-developed bus and metro systems, with Quito and Guayaquil having metro networks. Bus tickets can be purchased for as low as $0.25 for short distances within a city, while intercity bus fares range from $5 to $20, depending on the distance.

By Taxi:
Taxis are prevalent in urban areas, and radio taxis provide a convenient option for transportation. Metered taxi fares start at around $1, and additional charges apply based on distance. A typical short city ride may cost between $3 and $5.

By Train:
While Ecuador does not have an extensive train network, services like Tren Ecuador offer unique and scenic train journeys. Prices for train rides vary, with scenic excursions ranging from $20 to $50, depending on the route and duration.

By Car:
Ecuador's road network is well-developed, offering scenic routes and easy access to various destinations. Rental car prices start at around $30 per day for a basic compact car, while larger vehicles or premium models may cost $50 or more per day. Toll expenses on certain routes should also be considered.

By Motorcycle and Scooter:
Motorcycles and scooters are popular for navigating urban areas and exploring regions with dense traffic. Rental prices for motorcycles start at $20 per day, with scooters available for as low as $15 per day.
Renting a Vehicle:
If you choose to rent a car, ensure you meet the requirements. A valid driver's license, ID or passport, and a credit card are typically necessary. The rental cost for a standard car ranges from $30 to $80 per day, depending on the vehicle type and rental duration.

Ecuador's transportation options cater to various preferences, offering an opportunity to explore the country's unique geography, biodiversity, and cultural richness with options that fit different budget ranges. Whether you're traversing the Andes, visiting the Amazon rainforest, or enjoying the coastal beauty, Ecuador's diverse transportation infrastructure enhances your travel experience.

Copyright and Disclaimer:

Images Source:

Pixbay: (https://pixabay.com/)

All images' rights belong to their respective owners.

For detailed image licensing terms and conditions, kindly refer to the respective image sites' licensing terms and conditions.

Disclaimer:

This disclaimer is hereby presented to inform users of the "Ecuador Travel Guide" (henceforth referred to as "the Guide") of the terms and conditions of its use. By accessing or using this travel guide, you agree to the following conditions:

1. General Information: The Guide is created for informational purposes and offers travel-related content and advice related to Ecuador. It aims to provide general information and suggestions, which may not always be up to date. It is not a substitute for professional travel advice.

2. Accuracy of Information: While we strive to provide accurate and current information, we make no representations or warranties of any kind, expressed or implied, about the completeness, accuracy, reliability, suitability, or availability of the information, products, services, or related graphics contained in the Guide. Users should verify information independently before relying on it.

3. Liability Disclaimer: The author and the publisher of this Guide will not be liable for any loss or damage, including but not limited to indirect or consequential loss or damage, or any loss or damage whatsoever arising from loss of data or profits arising out of, or in connection with, the use of this Guide.

4. Third-Party Content: The Guide may include links to third-party websites or services related to Ecuador. We have no control over the nature, content, and availability of these sites and services. Inclusion of any links does not imply a recommendation or endorsement of the views expressed within them.

5. Safety and Legal Compliance: It is the user's responsibility to exercise caution, act in accordance with local laws and regulations, and ensure personal safety when engaging in any suggested activities or traveling in Ecuador.

6. Personal Responsibility: Users are solely responsible for their decisions and actions based on the information and advice provided in this Guide. The author and the publisher are not responsible for users' choices or outcomes related to travel or other activities in Ecuador.

By accessing or using this Ecuador Travel Guide, you agree to be bound by this disclaimer. If you disagree with any part of these terms and conditions, you are not allowed to use this Guide.

Milton Keynes UK
Ingram Content Group UK Ltd.
UKHW020840301123
433406UK00011B/138